At the Vet

A Division of The **McGraw·Hill** Companies

Columbus, Ohio

www.sra4kids.com

SRA/McGraw-Hill

*A Division of The **McGraw·Hill** Companies*

Copyright © 2002 by SRA/McGraw-Hill.

All rights reserved. Except as permitted under the United States Copyright Act, no part of this publication may be reproduced or distributed in any form or by any means, or stored in a database or retrieval system, without prior written permission from the publisher.

Printed in the United States of America.

Send all inquiries to:
SRA/McGraw-Hill
8787 Orion Place
Columbus, OH 43240-4027

ISBN 0-07-569731-9

3 4 5 6 7 8 9 DBH 05 04 03 02

Val has two pet cats.
Velvet is a black cat.
Vic is a gold cat.

Velvet and Vic are sick today.
Val must take her cats to a vet.
Val tells her cats, "I will put on a red vest.
Then we will go in the van."

They ride in Val's van.
Velvet likes the vet.
Vic does not like the vet.
He hides in the back of Val's van.

Dr. Kim looks at Velvet and Vic.
She states, "The cats ate a bad vine.
It made them sick."
She gives them some big white pills.

Val thanks Dr. Kim and says,
"I am glad I came.
Velvet and Vic will get well."

Val, Velvet, and Vic get in Val's van.
The vet helped Velvet and Vic get better.
Val can have fun with her cats again!